Common Ground

Photographs of
Rural and Small Town Life

by Raymond Bial

edited by Linda LaPuma Bial

Stormline Press, Inc. / Urbana, Illinois / 1986

Copyright © 1986 by Raymond Bial

All rights reserved. Except for the purpose of a brief review, no part of this book may be reproduced in any form without permission in writing from the author.

Library of Congress Catalog Card Number: 85-063625
International Standard Book Number: 0-935153-01-2

Stormline Press, Inc.
Post Office Box 593
Urbana Illinois 61801

This publication is made possible in part by a grant from the Illinois Humanities Council and the National Endowment for the Humanities.

Preface

It has been eight years since that fall day I traveled my first two-lane blacktop down a section line in east central Illinois, through the tunnels of corn that brought to my mind the subways of the city. Born and raised in Chicago, I had no idea that corn grew so high, no understanding of life on the prairie. I have since discovered how quiet "quiet" can be in the evening, watching the sun go down over miles of farmland. And I will forever remember the feeling of "prairie flying" through the newly harvested fields each autumn, on my way to meetings and gatherings in the many Parkland communities that have participated in our Community Arts Program.

Through my closest college friends, who had married and returned to the family farm after graduation, and the wonderful, warm people in Parkland's rural district, I have come to realize what life on the farm means to families, communities, and the world as a whole. Through the seasons and the years I have watched my friends struggle with the realities of their daily existence. My visits to the farm and my work in rural arts development have taught me how complex and risky the "simple life" has become. Interest rates, market prices, and production costs are constant concerns in a family's daily routine. Hearing the engines of low-flying airplanes dusting the fields, sending out well water to be tested, and cutting down an old tree to make room for a satellite dish are less common, but no less vivid, reminders that farm life has changed drastically.

It is my hope that *Common Ground* will provide recognition for the hardships and encourage celebration of the values of rural life in America. Such recognition and celebration are the driving forces, the philosophy, behind the Community Arts Program at Parkland College. In our sponsorship of this project, we hope we have provided a valuable service to a uniquely American culture.

Sheila Z. Beebe
Parkland College
March 1986

Introduction

This collection of photographs has grown out of my love for the farms and small towns of America, particularly around my home in east central Illinois. Having spent a good portion of my childhood in a small town in southern Indiana, then later on farms in Michigan and Illinois, I have always appreciated the special qualities of rural life.

I first realized how much I missed the farms and small towns of the Midwest when, having graduated from the University of Illinois, I went to work in a larger city on the East coast. When I came home for Christmas in 1971 I drove around the Illinois countryside drawn not just by the familiarity of the region, but by the extent of the changes which had occurred in just the few years since I'd left for college.

My first photograph was of a barn riddled by the wind and snow. Thereafter, on every visit home I took random drives through the countryside, mostly just looking around, but occasionally making a photograph – of fence posts stacked in a woodlot, of gas pumps in front of a grocery store, of a broken cafe window. These first photographs were in color, but I quickly came to appreciate black and white images, principally the ability of contrast, tonal range, and the interplay of light and shadow to communicate a distinct mood.

Two years later, after a short stint in graduate school, I was back home photographing regularly. At first I photographed simply what interested me without any conscious objective, let alone a philosophical basis for my work. Gradually I realized that I was photographing what I considered vestiges of the rural landscape – barns, grain elevators, farm implements, store fronts – all of which I saw disappearing in central Illinois and Indiana. From the start I was most interested in the subjects of my photographs and only secondarily in the technical aspects of the craft. I ended up teaching myself photography along the way.

On a very personal level I wanted to photograph what was left of the rural landscape I had known as a young man. Although the photographs have documentary elements, in no way have I ever considered them to be literal depictions. I have been most interested in achieving a certain feeling which many of us have about rural areas. One cannot pass an abandoned farmhouse without wondering with a certain melancholy about its history. Who had lived there? What celebrations, tragedies, and other poignant moments occurred within its walls? How did it come to be abandoned?

The plains may seem a flat, parsimonious landscape, but one can still look closely at Queen Anne's lace bobbing in the wind, black-eyed susans staring back at the sun, and blue chicory gracing the road shoulder. There are also lovely, worn textures in old buildings, fence rows, and other indications of human settlement of years ago which to me give this region its unique character.

In this sense the photographs aspire to art, with significant content, not just because they are carefully crafted, but because they are intended (1) to evoke certain feelings and (2) to act as generalizing symbols of how we would like to view rural areas as much as the reality of life in these regions. I happen to believe very strongly that the integrity of the individual will not be preserved unless we also retain unique ethnic and regional traits. To me it is these qualities which give flavor to our culture as a whole.

Initially I photographed only artifacts, but eventually began to make portraits of interesting people I encountered on day trips. I quickly cultivated a straightforward style which I think is quite true to the character of the people I was photographing, all of whom dressed quite naturally and approached the camera in the most unassuming manner. In the course of this part-time study of the past fourteen years I have made a couple of longer trips through the South and New England, particularly Maine, and curiously was able to photograph the same universal qualities of rural life. A few of the photographs in this book were made in Kentucky, Tennessee, Georgia, and Maine, as well as Illinois and Indiana. I am currently making photographs, particularly portraits, in small towns in central Illinois and Indiana, many of which are either disappearing or growing so large that they have lost their unique qualities. I have been especially interested in grocery stores and cafes which in many ways act as gathering places for people in small towns.

I hope that this selection of photographs will help us to better see ourselves, our homes, and other cultural features valued by people in the Midwest and in rural areas throughout the country.

Raymond Bial

Acknowledgments

I would like to thank the Illinois Humanities Council and the National Endowment for the Humanities whose support made this publication possible. I would also like to extend my warmest thanks to Robert Sutton and John Hoffman for their enthusiastic assistance with the project, to the humanists who participated in the public programs, and to the people I have known briefly yet enduringly through these photographs.

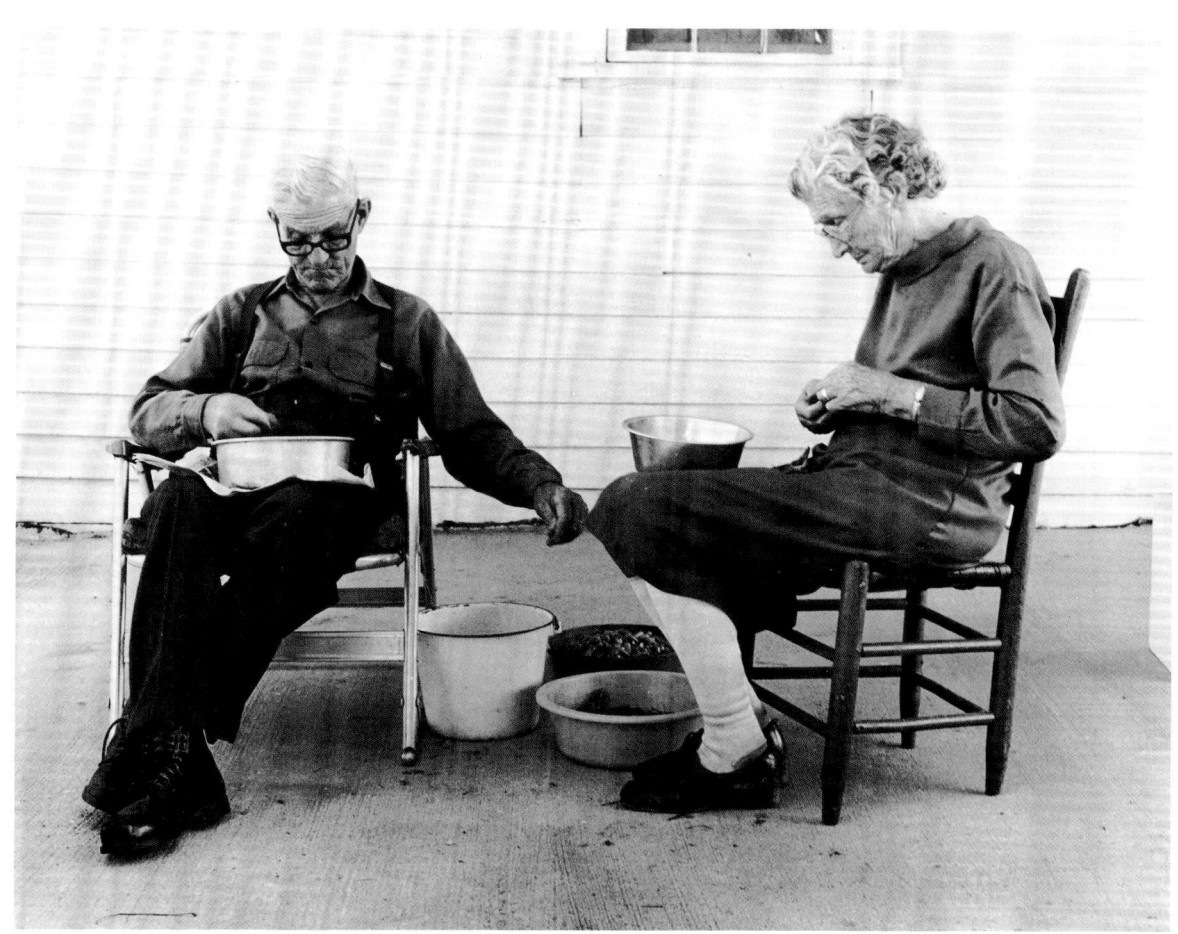

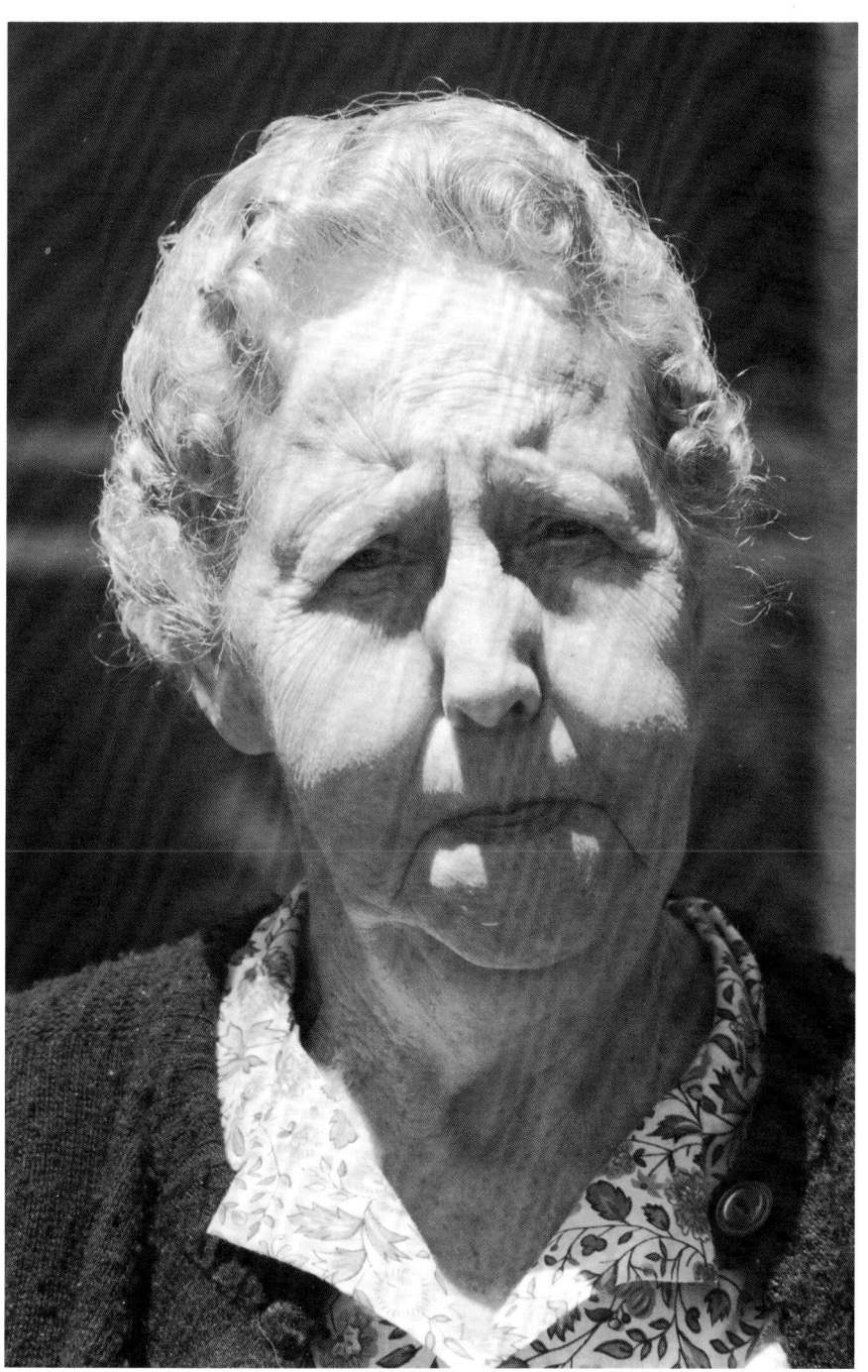

Reach for **SALLY ANN BREAD**

The photographs in this book were made on Ilford Pan F film and printed on Ilford Ilfobrom and Galerie papers by Raymond Bial.

The design and typography are by Four·C / IntelliText, Champaign Illinois.

The halftones and printing are by Andromeda Printing and Graphic Arts, Champaign Illinois.